WALK WITH ME THROUGH THE VOICE OF POETRY

Lydia Carolyn Willoughby

WESTBOW
PRESS®
A DIVISION OF THOMAS NELSON
& ZONDERVAN

Scripture taken from the King James Version of the Bible.

WestBow Press books may be ordered through booksellers or by contacting:

WestBow Press
A Division of Thomas Nelson & Zondervan
1663 Liberty Drive
Bloomington, IN 47403
www.westbowpress.com
1 (866) 928-1240

ISBN: 978-1-5127-1944-4 (sc)
ISBN: 978-1-5127-1943-7 (e)

Library of Congress Control Number: 2015918865

Print information available on the last page.

WestBow Press rev. date: 11/24/2015

CONTENTS

OUR REFLECTION TO OTHERS

The outcome of each challenge
Shows how well we take control.
Our actions are like a picture
And a reflection of our soul.

Negative actions based on emotions
Are never the better way.
They can result in hurting others,
Especially the words we say.

Acknowledging God's Holy Presence,
Letting His light through us show,
Allowing that light to be a testimony
Everywhere we go.

Our lives preach a sermon,
One that never lies.
We want to be a reflection of Jesus
Right before the world's eyes.

Being kind always to others
Should be our constant prayer,
That we may shine for Jesus
A reflection of Him everywhere.

Written by
Lydia Carolyn Willoughby
© 2012

Matthew 5:16
"Let your light so shine before men,
that they may see your good works,
And glorify your father which is in heaven."

SANTA AND Y2K

Santa was preoccupied
Sitting at his computer every day.
He was not getting ready for Christmas;
He was worried about Y2K.

His computer was not up to date.
He was wondering what to do.
He didn't know how to fix it.
Poor Santa didn't have a clue.

Some children faxed him letters
For toys they needed Christmas Day,
But his fax machine was not working.
He said to fix it, there was no way.

In the middle of November
He was still fooling with computer keys.
He wasn't feeling the greatest;
He spoke of arthritis in his knees.

He should have been getting his sled ready
And his reindeer fit and in swing,
Packing his sack for Christmas
But instead he hadn't done a thing.

I feel so sorry for Santa,
Our hero for Christmas Day;
He worried so much about the year 2000
And about Y2K.

This is now the year two thousand and fourteen.
Back then he was so tense
I sent letters and tried to reach him by phone,
But I haven't heard a word from him since.

Written by
Lydia Carolyn Willoughby
(11/16/99; 2014)

POOR SANTA

I wrote a letter to Santa;
I waited day after day.
After weeks of waiting
This is what he wrote to say.

Dear Lydia,

I received your letter. I checked each item and price, if you've been naughty, good, terrific or nice. I can't fulfill your wishes and I know it's a crying shame. Because of my bad credit I can't even live up to my name. I used to own some little stores and gave some things for free. Now my sack is empty, not a thing to put under the tree. My red suit is torn and ragged with patches on each side. When the kids come looking for me I have to run and hide.

I tried so hard to get a loan! It's embarrassing to go into town, especially knowing all the banks have turned me down. I checked my American Express, my Visa and Master Card, too. They have all reached the credit limit. I don't know what to do. I am sorry, Lydia.

I cannot help you, and from me and my reindeer, try to have a Merry Christmas. Maybe things will get better next year.

P.S. I forgot to mention I need a pair boots for the snow. I lost everything but my Jolly Spirit. Have a Happy Ho, Ho, Ho!

Love always,
Santa

Written by
Lydia Carolyn Willoughby
© December, 1992

WHAT CHRIST'S BIRTH MEANS TO ME

Out of a birth from divine simplicity
Came the dynamics of Christianity.
I decorate because I celebrate the birth of Christ,
The true meaning of Christmas.
His power is generated in us through his presence.
Many philosophers spend much time analyzing,
Criticizing, and comprehending the mysterious and
Miraculous power of His birth,
Yet they will never live
Long enough to fully understand it.
God's ways are past finding out.
Only in a heart that believes, He
demonstrates His power.
No time is left for me to dispute
which time of the year
Is truly His birth, whether it was in spring, summer,
Fall, or winter. The most important fact is that He
came to bring salvation to everyone that believes.
Theologians marvel at the divine
and religious truth of God.

Jesus Christ is a priceless gift
from our heavenly father.

Written by
Lydia Carolyn Willoughby
© 2012

Isaiah 9:6
"For unto us a child is born,
Unto us a son is given: and the government
Shall be upon His shoulder: and His name
Shall be called Wonderful, Counsellor;
The Mighty God, the Everlasting Father;
The Prince of Peace."

CHRISTMAS REFLECTION

Christmas is a time for reflection,
To show love and thankfulness,
Being inspired by our gift, the Lord Jesus,
Knowing that we are truly blessed.

I reflect on all the wonderful people
Giving God thanks every day.
For each person he put in my life,
That brightens up my way.

May this Christmas be real special.
When you look under your tree;
You'll find the gifts of thankfulness
And love to you from me.

Written by
Lydia Carolyn Willoughby
© 12/2/96

A CHRISTMAS POEM:
SHARING GIFTS

If you put a price on any gift,
It's really no gift at all.
For when it's given from the heart
It could be big or small.

Inspiration is the key
That causes us to share
With the people that we love
Who in our hearts are dear.

Giving is an act of love,
And this Christmas be a part
Of wrapping something special
That comes straight from the heart.

Written by
Lydia Carolyn Willoughby
© 12/20/95

GIVE THE GIFT OF LOVE

We spend lots and lots of dollars
On gifts we give and share.
We send lots of cards with greetings
To those we hold so dear.

The Christmas trees in all their splendor
With many presents on display,
Waiting for that special moment
To be opened on Christmas Day.

This Christmas you can make a difference,
First, by asking God above,
How you can give the most precious present,
The gift of unconditional love.

One way to give love is helping the homeless,
Giving a gift of a meal or toy,
Sharing some time with someone that's lonely.
That is true love and the spirit of joy.

Love can be silent within us.
What good is it if we don't give it away?
So remember when you open your presents
Think of the love you share on Christmas Day.

Written by
Lydia Carolyn Willoughby
© 12/11/1993

KEEPING CHRIST IN CHRISTMAS

How could there be a Christmas
And think it all so right,
To celebrate the season
Without the brightest light?

The decorations and shopping
Hearing about Santa and his reindeer,
I will not have true Christmas joy
If Jesus isn't here.

His birth is why I celebrate
His blood on Calvary,
And when I see the beautiful lights
I think of His love for me.

I bless and give Him thanks each day
For hope that helps along the way,
So with all the shopping, the rush and fuss
Remember the true reason of Christmas.

Written by
Lydia Carolyn Willoughby
© 2013

THE BLIZZARD OF '93

One of my birthdays will be remembered
Throughout history,
For it was the blizzard
Of 1993.
As I looked out my window
While the howling winds did blow,
Everything was covered
Under a blanket of snow.
It was my birthday.
I wished to go out on a date,
Or have some friends over
So we could celebrate.
Instead, alone I lit a few candles,
While the blizzard of '93
Hurled its devastation,
I sang, "Happy Birthday" to me.

Written by
Lydia Carolyn Willoughby
© 3/13/93

BEFORE I MET YOU

Before I met you
The world was such a lonely place,
It was not easy keeping
A smile on my face.
My life was an empty room.
I touched the walls with my tears.
In my heart was a gloom
Before I met you.
I hoped through all my spring times,
Dreary summers, too,
Falls and winters all alone
Before I met you.
Love songs used to make me cry
Their lyrics and their tunes.
I made my wish upon a star
And gazed alone at the moon.
It doesn't matter those lonely years;
Now you've come into my emptiness.
I can't believe it's true:
The laughter and the joy that came
Since I met you.

The world is a different place
More beautiful than the world I knew.
Words can't explain just how I feel;
It's a joy to be with you.

Written by
Lydia Carolyn Willoughby
© 6/23/96

AMERICA'S DARKEST DAY

We all watched in horror,
Staring in dismay;
September 11, 2001,
Was America's darkest day.

The sun was shining brightly.
New York's skies looked so clear.
Then suddenly evil came
Leaving us in deep despair.

Words fall short of description
Of the horror that was left behind;
Endurance of pain from tragedy,
Image of terror was our state of mind.

Time will heal our wounded hearts
For lost lives we still regret,
But through the years of time ahead,
This we will never forget.

Written by
Lydia Carolyn Willoughby
© 10/05/01

MY MERMAID FRIEND LUCY

What swam ashore to my surprise
With the most beautiful dazzling eyes,
I couldn't believe that my eyes did see
A lovely mermaid named Lucy.

The land was to her a very strange place,
Yet the smile she wore lit up her face.
She said, "Hey, there. My name is Lucy,"
Before she hastened back to the sea.

She rolled around on the sand
Then flapped her tail and waved her hand.
She swam away far from the shore
'Til I couldn't see her anymore.

I walked on the beach and sat by the bay,
Hoping I'd see her swimming someday.
Upon the ocean front I'd be
Looking through each wave for my friend Lucy.

Her visit was so very brief.
I ponder yet in disbelief;
Was it a dream? If not, it never fails,
For I still believe in fairytales.

Written by
Lydia Carolyn Willoughby
© 07/05/97

MAN AND THE RATTLE SNAKE

I am a rattle snake.
Get out of my way.
I am looking for my food
So I won't starve today.

I'd rather save my venom;
That's what I want to do.
My venom is precious.
Why should I waste it on you?

I crawl on my belly;
I crawl up the tree.
You buy your food in stores;
You're more fortunate than me.

So when you hear me rattle
I am only trying to say,
I am in search of my food,
So get out of my way.

Written by
Lydia Carolyn Willoughby
© 11/18/00

THE SNOWY OWL

In a tree near my window
Stood an owl that I could see,
With eyes bright and shining
Gazing right back at me.
Everywhere covered with snow
The winter skies so gray,
But those eyes were filled with sunshine;
Then I watched it fly away.
That was a precious moment
And through the snow, sleet and rain
I look for that owl in the tree
Wishing to see it again.

Written by
Lydia Carolyn Willoughby
© 2/24/07

MY BEAUTIFUL CAT, SNOW WHITE

Snow White's fur is so beautiful,
The most gorgeous cat I've ever seen,
The kind of cat I always hoped for,
With eyes so big and green.

She has so much love for me;
I can see it in those eyes.
She enjoys her meals she loves to eat.
You can tell by her size.

Her purr to me is special;
Words she likes to say.
I know she says, "I love you."
I hear it every day.

I love her very dearly.
Some things in life to be are meant.
She is my fury angel;
To me was heaven sent.

Written by
Lydia Carolyn Willoughby
© 5/4/14

PLEASE DO NOT FORGET

From my beautiful pet cat Sweetie
who passed away 11/27/03

Do not forget me.
Keep me always in your memory.
Remember how I used to purr
And how soft and silky was my fur.

Remember how I would lie on the bathroom rug,
Waiting for you to get out of the tub.
Watching you leave for work was no fun,
So I sat at the patio door and enjoyed the sun.

I would wait every evening at the door for you
Just being a friend loving and true.
You would always so gently pat my head,
And I cuddled next to you at night in bed.

I was around you most of the time.
When I felt ignored I would meow and whine.
I have taken this love for you deep in my heart.
It's very sad now that we are apart.

I admit sometimes I was a pest,
But you still loved me 'cause you are the best.
I enjoyed your piano music; I thought it was sweet.
Though I didn't have hands, I
applauded with my feet.

So from the animal heaven, this I had to do.
I sent this poem especially for you.
That's because I know I was a wonderful pet
And for that reason, don't ever FORGET.
Love,
Sweetie

Written by
Lydia Carolyn Willoughby
© 1/04/04

THE FRIGHTENED OWL

An owl that lived high in a tree
Lost his way 'til he could not see.
He tried to fly while still daylight,
But the sun's bright ray impaired his sight.

It got dark, and he became afraid.
Realizing the mistake he had made,
Feeling sad and down on his luck.
He was in the street and got hit by a truck.

The poor bird got stuck in the grill.
He could not move, so he stood still,
His piercing yellow eyes peering from there
Filling those around with fear.

They wondered, "What in the world is that?
It's not a dog; it's not a cat."
They then realized it's a feathered fowl,
Nothing other than a frightened owl.

Someone from the Florida Wildlife came;
He was rescued with such worldwide fame.
It's said that owls are known to be wise,
But I know they wouldn't forget
those big yellow eyes.

Written by
Lydia Carolyn Willoughby
© 5/19/13

THE DOOR IN THE WALL

The door in the wall is the dark before dawn.
The end of despair that lights a new morn,
Its hidden years of glory
Its treasures are sealed;
But search and you'll find it;
Its secret's to be revealed.
Like at the end of a rainbow, skies are blue;
In your wall of wonder is a hidden door for you.
Your time and your patience
To search high and low,
Perseverance and courage
Will lead you to that door.
Whatever life offers, take heed to your call.
Somewhere in your heart is the door in the wall.

Written by
Lydia Carolyn Willoughby
© 7/25/94

MY PAINFUL DIVORCE

I thought I married my best friend,
With hopes our love would never end.
So many years of bliss and joy;
Now my heart to you is just a toy.
Together I thought we would grow old;
Your heart towards me has turned cold.
I am left in the world sad and alone
With no sweetheart or darling to call my own.
The scorn of rejection is oh, so real.
I wonder how could our marriage fail.
I haven't any more tears to cry;
I want so much to live but feel to die.
A part of me is no longer there.
What hurts the most? You no longer care.
You were so loving; now you are mean.
I wish what's happened were all a dream.
If I could turn back the clock's hand of time
When you were so sweet, so loving, and kind.
This in the future I never could see,
That someone else has taken the place of me.
I must find some light in this dark place,

Even when I see pictures of your face.
I'll take the high road looking each day above.
Is there such a thing as falling out of love?
You were treasured in my heart where still a bond;
Time I know will heal. Now I must move on.

Written by
Lydia Carolyn Willoughby
© 11/11/13

CINDERELLA

I have a date and I am late.
My name is Cinderella.
I know I'll have fun
So I have to run
To be on time to meet my fellow.

I've been left behind
And that's all the time.
I never had a fair chance.
I've always been alone
Doing the chores at home.
Now it's my time to dance.

I wished and hoped.
I cried and moped,
Still trying to lift my self-esteem.
While I mopped the floors
Behind slammed doors
I still had my Cinderella dream.

Every night I cried in my bed,
My eyes always red.
Tears I cried to God and not another.
My wait was so long,
But in my heart was a love song.
Now my prince is my true love forever.

Written by
Lydia Carolyn Willoughby
© 2/24/01

THE POWER IN A SMILE

Like flowers, how they flourish and bloom,
A radiant smile can scatter gloom,
Making the universe brighter to see.
Let a smile begin with you and me.
Its beauty attracts anywhere, any place,
Like gifts exchanging from each face.
A smile can say a lot; though it's not heard,
It speaks but not with a spoken word.
Too bad everyone wouldn't feel this way,
But I'll still share smiles every day.
They're bright as the sun and wide as the sea.
I wish the whole world could smile with me.

Written by
Lydia Carolyn Willoughby
© 7/29/95

YESTERDAY'S LAST NIGHT

I will not go through again
A yesterday's last night.
I tossed and turned. The clock, "Tick, tock,"
With no morning yet in sight.

I felt too sad to even cry.
Wrapped up in my gloom,
I could hear the sound of crickets
While darkness filled my room.

I ponder on my latter years,
And wish the future I could see.
Is one chosen to be my true love?
Or if lonely shall I be?

So still was every minute;
Cold and frigid were my feet.
Long and dreary were the hours;
Alone I listened to my heart beat.

I will not spend another moment
Of terror's lonely flight,
How doomed the thoughts and real the fear
Of Yesterday's Last Night.

Written by
Lydia Carolyn Willoughby
© 6/27/05

A SLAVE'S PRAYER

(1)
Way beneath the blazing sun
In yonder's dreary field
I worked my fingers to the bone
Where often I would kneel.

(2)
My weary knees would cease to rise
Above my aching sore,
Then look to God for little strength
To work, the fields endure.

(3)
With sweat some days to quench my thirst
And wonder who to blame
For all the agony I face,
So cruel: intolerable pain.

(4)
I gazed the deep blue skies above
And often I would pray,
Why God, for such injustice done
And hardship led the way.

(5)
The years rolled on my wrinkled skin.
My failing eyes did see,
That I, a slave, through all my prayer
Have seen the day set free.

Written by
Lydia Carolyn Willoughby
© 09/16/87

Psalms 116: 1, 2
1. "I love the Lord, because He hath heard
my voice and my supplications.
2. Because He hath inclined His ear unto me,
therefore will I call upon Him as long as I live."

A PRAYER

Eternal God in whom our hope
and destiny are instituted,
Affirm the good in every negative situation,
So that we can focus on our faith in thee.
Help us to reach out to those who are less
Fortunate, that they may see your light in us.
Help us to reach our goals and fulfill our purpose.

Let us be aware that life's journey is just
A preparation for our final destination,
Which one day we will discover with thee
When we live the life of faith.
Keep us always in your loving care. Amen.

Written by
Lydia Carolyn Willoughby
© 1/8/93

A THANKSGIVING DAY PRAYER

Dear God, we give thee thanks today
For everything you made.
We give thee thanks for all this food
On this table laid.
Lord, those who do not have,
We know for them you care.
Let them know you will provide
And give us hearts to share.
As we partake, let it do us good
This day, our hearts we pray.
Let us always be thankful
Knowing Thanksgiving is every day.

Written by
Lydia Carolyn Willoughby
© 1985

Psalm 107:1
"Oh, give thanks unto the Lord,
for He is good; for His mercy
endureth forever."

A PRAYER

Lord, with nowhere else to go
I face a great, red sea.
I have looked in all directions,
But my help must come from thee.
Never have you failed me,
And I know you never will.
You always fought my battles
While I believed your word
And stood still.
Thank you for this answered prayer.
In your presence I humbly bow.
By faith I receive this blessing.
You will make a way somehow.

Written by
Lydia Carolyn Willoughby
© 1985

A PRAYER:
STRENGTH FOR A NEW DAY

Lord, I am feeling tired.
My feet from standing hurt.
I feel drained and weary
From a long, hard day at work.
Thank you for the job you've provided.
I try to do my best.
Your word is my comfort
As I lie down to rest.
I know that you supply my needs
From your abundance above
I have blessed assurance
From your abiding love.
Forgive me for wrong I've said or done.

These words I humbly pray,
Thank you, Lord, for everything
As you give strength for a new day.

Written by
Lydia Carolyn Willoughby
© 1985

Psalm 29: 11
"The Lord will give strength unto His people;
The Lord will bless His people with peace."

A PRAYER:
THE EAGLE'S PRAYER

Dear God, you gave me special wings
So I can scale the skies.
I cannot fly with other birds
For I must soar high.

My faith in you to use my wings
Is when I put you first.
Thanks for these eyes that I can see
To explore the universe.

Sometimes I feel a little lonely
And ask the question, "Why?"
But God, you often let me know
Where I go, other birds can't fly.

When the storms are approaching
I am not afraid when dark clouds form;
The updraft keeps me way above.
I conquer every storm.

I am unique in all creation,
Representing strength and courage, too.
Thank you, Lord, for the ability
To succeed in all I do. Amen

Written by
Lydia Carolyn Willoughby
© 1/29/04

Isaiah 40: 31
"But they that wait upon the Lord
Shall renew their strength; they shall
Mount up with wings as eagles, they shall run
And not be weary, and they shall
walk, and not faint."

HOUSE WARMING PRAYER

Thank you, Lord, for this home you have given.
Fill it with your presence and wealth.
Grant us peace as we reside here
With good neighbors, joy and good health.

Let it be a house of worship,
A place to spend time every day,
In reading your word for truth and guidance
So that we can show others the way.

Let each room be bright and cheerful
With Jesus always a welcomed guest.
Let its shine be like a lighthouse:
Our palace, our castle and haven of rest.

May the windows and doors be always covered
With God's protection from above,
When family and friends stop by to visit
Give them always the warmth of your love. Amen

Written by
Lydia Carolyn Willoughby
© 08/12/11

Proverbs 12:7
"The wicked are overthrown and are not:
But the house of the righteous shall stand."

A PRAYER:
A NEW DAY'S PRAYER

Great God of this universe and all men,
Thank you for another day granted to me.
Thank you for yesterday, I trust I have
Used its time wisely, for it will
never return to me again.
Now I look toward your holy hill.
Give me new insight, new vision,
and new aspirations.
I refuse to settle for where I am.
Your vision for me is much greater than I can see.
You are the only one that can help
me accomplish all my dreams.
Father, remove the scales from my eyes so

That blurry vision will be clear.
Give me the courage to step toward new, open doors.
Amen.

Written by
Lydia Carolyn Willoughby
© 5/30/13

Philippians 4:13
*"I can do all things through Christ
which strengtheneth me."*

A PRAYER:
HELP ME, LORD

Lord, help me to be a flower
On someone's gloomy day;
Help me to be sunshine
When someone's skies turn gray.

Help me to give some water
To quench someone's thirst;
Help me to live my purpose
Anywhere in the universe.

Help me to be a rainbow
When floods have caused some pain,
So I can be a reminder
That the sun will shine again.

Lord, help me to bring some happiness
When a soul has been cast down.
Help me to cause someone to wear
A smile instead of a frown.

And when I feel sad and low
And my blue skies turn gray,
I know, Lord, you'll be the one
To brighten up my way. Amen.

Written by
Lydia Carolyn Willoughby
© 1993

A PRAYER FOR GOD'S PROTECTION
FATHER, WITH THY HAND

When this world of pain and suffering
Often leaves us in despair,
Father, with thy hand lead us.
Help us not to faint or fear
When in trouble sore and grievous
Heavy hearts laiden with pain.
Father, with thy hand uplift us
When we call upon your name.
When in sorrow we are weeping
You are acquainted with each fallen tear,
And however we are feeling,
Keep us in your loving care.
When by danger we are surrounded

And cannot see nor understand,
Keep us, Lord, from harm and danger.
Protect with thy mighty hand. Amen

Written by
Lydia Carolyn Willoughby
© 1985

A PRAYER:
BAD HABITS

Father, I have some bad habits
Which have strong control of me.
I have struggled a long time with them,
Father; now I turn to thee.
With these habits I feel guilty.
Lord, only you can set me free
Over these habits. I am asking,
Give me complete victory.
Thank you, Lord, for listening to me.
Now with you I feel at peace;
Give me power to overcome
As these habits I release.

Written by
Lydia Carolyn Willoughby
© 1985

Psalm 19: 12-13
"Who can understand his errors?
Cleanse thou me from secret faults.

Keep back thy servant also from presumptuous sins;
Let them not have dominion over
me: then shall I be upright,
And I shall be innocent from the
great transgression."

MY PRAYER CLOSET

I love to spend time with my heavenly Father
For I believe Jesus is coming soon.
I need to get closer to Him
In my prayer closet, my upper room.

So sweet and precious are those moments
When I am quiet and alone.
In my secret room where I worship
Is a special place in my home.

There are some things I cannot tell others
When from the busy world I hide,
But I know I can tell everything to Jesus.
Truly in Him I can confide.

Heaven is real; it comes down before me.
That's when the spirit takes control.
In my prayer closet with my heavenly father
Is where he richly blesses my soul.

Written by
Lydia Carolyn Willoughby
© 1984

Matthew 6:6
*"But thou, when thou prayest, enter into thy closet,
and when thou hast shut thy door, pray to thy father
which is in secret; and thy father
which seeth in secret
shall reward thee openly."*

A PRAYER TO GET OUT OF DEBT

Help me, Lord, I am in debt,
Frustrated that I haven't paid off these bills yet.
When I didn't have the cash, I used my credit card,
Struggling to make ends meet in times that are hard.
I must confess without a doubt,
I brought some things I could have done without.
I tried to make things better, but
instead they got worse.
Credit card spending can become a curse.
Father, you said you'll supply every need,
But sometimes as humans, we
get caught up with greed.
Have mercy on me; I know you will
Help me to find a way to pay off each bill.
And when I have done so, a desire I must fulfill,
Lord, give me financial wisdom and
a made up mind and will,

Never again to be tempted or let
Myself be ever found in a sad state of DEBT.

Written by
Lydia Carolyn Willoughby
© 12/29/12

THE LORD'S PRAYER

Matthew 6: 9-13
"Our father which art in heaven,
Hallowed by thy name.
Thy Kingdom come, thy will be done
In earth as it is in heaven.
Give us this day our daily bread.
And forgive us our debts, as we forgive our debtors.
And lead us not into temptation, but
Deliver us from evil: for thine is the Kingdom,
And the power, and the glory,
Forever. Amen."

A PRAYER

Dear God, your existence is unsearchable.
Your place, everywhere, and
time is countless to thee.
We lift our hearts in reverence to your
Excellence which is on earth and above.
By faith we acknowledge your unseen
Countenance, your creation is seen throughout time.
Fill us with your Holy Spirit that we will
Be able to perform our earthly duties
with dignity and grace.
Fill us with your love and peace
Both now and forevermore. Amen

Written by
Lydia Carolyn Willoughby
© 01/18/93

Psalm 8:1
"O Lord our Lord, how excellent
is thy name in all the earth!
Who has thy glory above the heavens"

THE PROMISE FULFILLED

One day in disgrace and dishonor
Jesus walked a dusty road,
Carrying the cross as He tripped and stumbled
To Calvary, He went with a heavy load.

They mocked and scorned and spat on Him.
His heart must have bled that day,
Only because He obeyed His father,
Yet for those people He breathed a prayer.

Father, forgive, for they do not know
The real reason why I came;
Father, with your love and mercy
Look this day upon my shame.

Think of the agony as those nails were driven.
Think of the sword that pierced His side,
And those thorns as they were placed on His head.
Think of that day Christ was crucified.

The stripes on His back were sore and painful,
But He bore them with dignity and grace,
Because He knew those stripes to Him given
Would one day heal people from every race.

It's time the world turns to this wonderful savior
And from their wickedness and pride,
To give God all the praise and honor
For sending Jesus Christ who died.

Jesus, you couldn't have done it
Without God's strength and divine will.
You bore it all 'til it was finished.
Thank you, heavenly Father,
for the promise fulfilled.

Written by
Lydia Carolyn Willoughby
© 1985

St. Luke 24: 44
"And He said unto them, 'These are the
words which I spake unto you,
While I was yet with you that all things
must be fulfilled, which were written
in the Law of Moses, and
In the prophets, and in the Psalms concerning me.'"

GOD'S ART WORK

I memorize a crystal stream
And embrace the fresh, clean air.
I review in my mind a horizon
And skies that are sunny and clear.

I rehearse the tunes that little birds sing,
Their voices melodious sweet;
I imagine walking by an ocean
With velvet sand under my feet.

I picture climbing high mountains
Looking down at green pastures below,
Or shining icicles in winter
And God's white blanket of snow.

This is a picture of God's perfect nature.
Oh, what a miraculous design,
To unfold it each day as my treasure,
A colorful picture in my mind.

I carry it through life's lonely pathways
And when my world is gloomy and gray,
It will always be a painting of sunshine
As I give praises to the artist each day.

Written by
Lydia Carolyn Willoughby
© 4/25/94

FALL

Looking out my window,
Fall is everywhere in view.
The trees with such beautiful colors
Beneath the autumn skies so blue.

Colors that are a part of the season:
Some green, red, yellow and gold.
Among fallen leaves are busy squirrels
Gathering food before it gets cold.

The breezes now cool and refreshing,
I love that chill in the air,
That feeling that winter is coming
And the holidays are getting near.

It's time to say so long to flowers
And the warm feeling they bring,
For now we'll enjoy the fall and winter
Until it's time to celebrate spring.

Written by
Lydia Carolyn Willoughby
© 1989

DEATH WITH HOPE

Our lives are only lent to us.
Death will come someday;
Sometimes we take life for granted
And forget we are not here to stay.

It's appointed for man once to die;
So will you, and so will I.
Death always brings us sorrow,
But there is hope and a brighter tomorrow.

On that morning when the clouds shall break
In death, our souls shall awake.
Jesus will come to the earth again
To take us where there's no sorrow or pain.

To dwell with him forevermore
On that beautiful heavenly shore,
Eternal life we will ever spend
With God our father, with Jesus, our friend.

Written by
Lydia Carolyn Willoughby
© 1975

Hebrews 9:27
*"And as it is appointed unto men once to
die, but after this the judgement:"*

MY TRUE VALENTINE

Jesus is my valentine.
He is the truest love of mine.
Through winter, fall, summer or spring
I never lack for anything.

The clouds He patterns way up high
Are to me love letters in the sky,
And stars at night like diamonds to see
His deepest love for you and me.

Like a box of candy with words so sweet
Full of wisdom and power, words so deep
A reminder for me to always know
The Bible, written long time ago.

His unconditional love is real.
This love for me will never fail.
The truest, dearest love of mine
Is Jesus, my everyday valentine.

Written by
Lydia Carolyn Willoughby
© 1987

John 3:16
*"For God so loved the world, that He
gave His only begotten son,
that whosoever believeth in Him should not perish,
but have everlasting life."*

BUMPS ON THE ROAD

Along life's path and journey
There are many bumps on the road,
They cause pain and heartache
When walking with a heavy load.
But as we walk with Jesus
And our faith we do not lose,
The way will become brighter
And the road will become smooth.

Written by
Lydia Carolyn Willoughby
© 2/7/13

COURAGE

Courage is not the absence of fear
But the willingness to act,
Even if we are afraid of what
Might happen when we do.
God cares and sends us Courage
To put our woes to flight,
For Courage is God's candle
That lights the darkest night.

By Gilbert

ROSA PARKS' COURAGE

It took one woman's courage
To be a part of history,
When black people were denied
Their freedom and liberty.

To sit on buses anywhere they chose
And not only at the back,
Rosa Parks took a stand for freedom
In the bus seat where she sat.

I sometimes have to wonder
How could the former leaders of this land
Allow such injustice to be done.
I cannot understand.

This all happened to show us
What faith and courage can do.
She changed the course for generations;
She made a dream come true.

A grim future became brighter.
She won a raging war,
A victory for the rights of black people;
That's what she sat for.

Let her always be an example
Of courage that defied fate.
Giving us freedom to choose our seats on buses,
A legacy, powerful and great.

Written by Lydia Carolyn Willoughby

GOD'S ANOINTED

When you are God's anointed
Some paths may seem not right.
He leads us through the valleys
Walking by faith and not by sight.

It may hurt to do the right thing
Trying hard to do the best,
But remaining faithful
Is the key to passing the test.

Joseph with his brothers
In their hearts he could not tell
That they could be so jealous of him
To thrust him into a well.

But little did they understand
That it was all God's plan,
For him to be sold as a slave,
To reach his promised land.

He was lied on and went to prison
But God's favor was with him there.
His gift that God had given
He used without a fear.

That gift made room for him
As he stood before the king
His heart of love and forgiveness
Made him ruler over many things.

To be anointed can be costly,
Travelling paths you don't understand.
Still, keep the faith; keep on believing
And you will reach your promised land.

Written by
Lydia Carolyn Willoughby
© 3/11/14

Proverbs 18: 16
*"A man's gift maketh room for Him,
And bringeth Him before great men."*

THE LOSS OF A TRUE MOTHER

A mother's life journey
When it comes to an end,
Leaves that feeling of emptiness,
The loss of a best friend.

That bond that's now broken
That void will ever be,
When a mother is gone
From the life of you and me.

With love and dedication
Her life filled with grace
Never to be another
Who can ever fill her place.

Her assignment as a mother
Was to be an angel, too,
To care for and guide us
As we journey our life through.

The joys of having a true mother,
Then the sorrow to see her go
Only those who have lost her
Will understand and know.

That a mother's love is forever
And time heals the pain,
But hope stays alive
That she will be seen again.

Written by
Lydia Carolyn Willoughby

FROM THE PIT TO THE PALACE

It's never fun being in the pit
When others can adjust, making
you feel like a misfit,
Having wings of an eagle but still cannot fly
Struggling to survive, not wanting to die.

It's tough to be there not seeing a way
Of soaring to a mountain and wanting to stay,
But a cry from the soul, a desire in the heart
And prayers of faith can be a new start.

At the end of a tunnel it's said there is light.
A pit can seem dark, but God's presence is bright
With a vision, a purpose and faith everyday
To lead to your palace that may not be far away.

Though you may be flat out on the pit's miry floor
When opportunity comes, you must answer the door.
Never hesitate for where grace is found.
In one split second, God can turn it around.

When delivered from a pit just look back to see
That a pit has a purpose, one for you and one for me.
If not yet delivered keep praising God still.
He is working out your purpose
according to His will.

It's never meant to be a permanent place
Just life's experiences as we run the Christian race,
Let your light shine; be always your best
Before you reach the palace, the pit is only a test.

Written by
Lydia Carolyn Willoughby
© 3/10/13

Psalm 40:1-2
*(1) I waited patiently for the Lord; and He
inclined unto me, and heard my cry.
(2) He brought me up also out of an horrible
pit, out of the miry clay, and set
my feet upon a rock, and established my goings.*

WE ARE NOT ALONE IN THE FIRE

Fires in life, when kindled by trials,
God can hinder them or He may allow;
He chooses to go through them with us.
He takes the heat away somehow.

Lest we are destroyed and be like ashes
Where we vanish and be no more
Friends and loved ones may flee and fail us
As troubles around us soar.

But there is a secret in the fire.
While passing through, it will unfold.
Those who faint not but still trust Jesus
Will come out better than the finest gold.

When the three Hebrew boys were
thrown in the furnace
Nebuchadnezzar thought they would be no more;
To his surprise when he looked in the furnace
He threw in three men but instead they were four.

The fires of life cannot destroy us.
God wants us to believe and know
That he can appear in the midst beside us
Like with Shadrach, Meshach and Abednego.

Written by
Lydia Carolyn Willoughby
© 1985

1 Corinthians 3:13
"Every man's work shall be made manifest:
For the day shall declare it, because
it shall be revealed by fire;
and the fire shall try every man's
work of what sort it is."

MY HUMBLE HOME

My home is my castle.
I thank God every day
For providing me with shelter;
It's where I love to pray.

In my kitchen I converse with him
As I prepare each meal.
In my bathroom I sing to him;
His presence I can feel.

In my living room he sits with me;
He is always my special guest.
In my bedroom I share my deepest thoughts
And he guards me as I rest.

Written by
Lydia Carolyn Willoughby
© 1991

MY REALITY BOOK

I was looking through the pages
In my reality book of life
When suddenly it dawned on me
That I was never a mother or wife.

So I continued to flip the pages
And all that I could see
Were chapters of my singleness
That kept staring back at me.

They were chapters of my struggles
And of my joys and happiness, too,
But the ones that stood out the most
Were the storms God brought me through.

In my many chapters,
My motto: Always to pray,
No matter what seems impossible;
God always makes a way.

My book is far from finished
With some chapters to recite,
So until my heavenly Father calls me home
There are many more chapters I'll write.

Written by
Lydia Carolyn Willoughby
© 5/20/14

This Acrostic was written for my sister's appreciation service at Whitepark Wesleyan Holiness Church, Barbados. 09/15/13

E is for Excellence; you strive for nothing less.

S is for Service; you give your very best.

T is for Trustworthy; you are reliable, dependable, and true.

H is for Honor; you honor the Lord in all you do.

E is for Ethical; how you live your life, it's seen.

And **R** is for Royal; you are named after a Queen.

Esther, these words are some of your descriptions, though they are a few.

Continue to be enriched with God's goodness, and remember, we all love you.

Written by
Lydia Carolyn Willoughby
© 9/6/13

GOD'S ANSWER IS THE BEST

With God all things are possible;
This we all should know:
Through prayer and believing
We'll help our faith to grow.

We may ask for a heart's desire
And for His answer maybe wait.
Just keep confessing His word everyday
For no blessing is ever late.

Though we may feel disappointed
When His answer to us is no,
He only wants for us what's good
Because He loves us so.

Trust Him, for every answer
Whether it's NO, WAIT or YES,
He is God all-knowing of everything
And for us He wants what's BEST.

Written by
Lydia Carolyn Willoughby
© 10/03/10

Psalms 84:11
*"For the Lord God is a sun and
shield: the Lord will give
grace and glory: no good thing will He
withhold from them that walk uprightly."*

BIRTH, LIFE, DEATH, GATEWAY TO ETERNITY

So snug inside a mother's womb
In walls of nature, dark and gloom,
Just like inside a shell, a pearl,
A baby prepares to enter the world.
Vulnerable to Mother's love and care
Life's hidden secrets its pathway to dare.
Has its pleasure, has its worth,
Brings light to life: a baby's birth.
And so from there the years will fly
With memories of that baby's first cry.
The beauty of life to seek its own
To journey to a future yet unknown.
God, our time didn't give but lend
For whichever age that life will end
To know He'll constantly be there
Through death's dark valley will be no fear
And when journeyed, that pathway of night,
Death's cold harsh secrets will soon be bright.

With Jesus our comfort a new world to see
That births the gateway to eternity.

Written by
Lydia Carolyn Willoughby
© 1997

PURPOSE

God gives life and purpose
That we are meant to fulfill,
No matter how many things befall us
Whatever he promised is His will.
All we have to do is follow,
Though the path may not be clear.
It's not what we see but to keep on believing
When faith is leading, there is no fear.
God doesn't dwell on age; he sees the purpose.
If we do not quit it will come to pass.
It's worth the wait, the toil and labor
To reach our destiny at last.

Written by
Lydia Carolyn Willoughby
© 2/25/14

CHAPTERS IN OUR BOOK

Life is made up of chapters
In every experience of our lives.
When we seek to know our purpose
Its knowledge will make us wise.

To reach any goal is a chapter
Whether they be many or few,
Living and learning teach experience;
Failures and mistakes are chapters, too.

Everyone has a story
Of life's journey in any season or stage,
But it's always a mystery and excitement
Whenever we begin a new page.

Disappointment, success, achievements, or loss
Whatever in life it took,
To reach where we are today
Are all chapters in our book.

Written by
Lydia Carolyn Willoughby
© 5/18/10

THE PASSING OF A LOVED ONE

My world is crushed, shattering my will,
A will that strengthened me to go on.
How do I say goodbye to someone I love
When we were together; now you are gone?

Words cannot express how I truly feel.
All I know I am cornered in a world of grief.
From pain and loneliness of missing you
I cannot find relief.

The stillness of each night holds memories of you;
I wish to wake up from a dream that's not true.
I long to hold you, to tell you how much I care.
I dread facing each day, knowing you are not here.

Dear Jesus, please hold me in your loving arms;
Comfort me through this dark night until dawn;
Carry me now while I am frail and weak
'Til I have the strength to carry on.

Written by
Lydia Carolyn Willoughby
© 2005

Psalm 31:24
*"Be of good courage, and He shall
strengthen your heart,
all ye that hope in the Lord."*

A SERVANT GIRL LIKE ME

A poor servant girl was I;
In bondage was my stay.
My work was never ended
But I prayed to God each day.

There were many lonely hours
I spent away from home,
Feeling so discouraged,
Forgotten and all alone.

Many times taken advantage of,
Harsh words were spoken to me,
But I kept trusting in Jesus
That one day He'll set me free.

When I prepared the table that
Before the rich was spread,
Unworthy was I to partake with them,
So alone I ate my daily bread.

But I know at the feast in heaven
We'll be all in one accord;
I'll be seated at that table
With my savior who is Lord.

They cared not for me as a human being,
Only for their silver and gold,
But God cares the world about me
Especially for my soul.

One day while washing the dishes
My soul felt very happy.
That day I started singing;
Then God spoke to me.

In Isaiah fourteen and verse three
I heard his voice so clear.
I'll give you rest from your sorrow
And from that hard bondage and fear.

The tears just fell from my eyes
I did not even know
A poor servant girl like me
How much God loves me so.

Written by
Lydia Carolyn Willoughby
© 1984

Isaiah 14:3
*"And it shall come to pass in the day that the Lord
Shall give thee rest from thy sorrow, and
from thy fear, and from the hard bondage
wherein thou wast made to serve."*

GOD'S APPOINTMENT

God's children are never disappointed;
Whatever an outcome may be,
We live by faith believing
And not by what we see.

He wants the best for his children
For He is faithful and wise;
What may seem like a disappointment
Is a blessing in disguise.

When God is in control
And things don't seem right to you,
Though it may seem like a disappointment
Here's what you should do.

Take the "D" off the word, "Disappointment,"
And instead add a capital "H."
Now what do you get? His "Appointment."
He does what's best for His children's sake.

Written by
Lydia Carolyn Willoughby
© 1985

Psalm 37: 4-5
*"Delight thyself also in the Lord; and He
shall give thee the desires of thine heart.
Commit thy way unto the Lord; trust also
in Him; and He shall bring it to pass."*

A RETIREMENT POEM:
MORE TEA TIME WITH JESUS

Life now without hustle and bustle
The life of stress now behind,
Pull up a chair; relax more with Jesus
For fellowship and have tea time.

More time to enjoy a beautiful sunrise
And a precious sunset, too,
Or a peaceful quiet walk somewhere
Admiring skies that are blue.

Each passing day may you feel His presence
Revived with life anew;
Enjoy life's tea time with Jesus
At a table spread for two.

Written by
Lydia Carolyn Willoughby
© 8/25/11

FOR THE PASSING OF MY PARENTS

Rev. and Mrs. Clyde Willoughby

Daddy
Sunrise: Dec. 20, 1907
Sunset: Oct. 15, 2004

Mummy
Sunrise: Oct. 13, 1923
Sunset: Sept. 19, 2004

You were both two special people
Whose candles shine so bright,
Candles in a world of darkness
Burning in the night.

Your lights were never hidden
So that everyone could see,
Living your lives for Jesus
Hand in hand throughout life's journey.

You were both such an inspiration.
Now there are two less flames,
Because you made such a difference
Our world hasn't been the same.

It's years since you've been home with Jesus
Who is our greatest light,
But in our hearts you'll always be
Those two candles burning bright.

Written by
Lydia Carolyn Willoughby
© 9/15/10

HOPE NOW IN GOD

Hopes, dreams and wishes
We look forward to coming true,
Working hard at pursuing them
In everything we do.

Our hopes and dreams differ;
Our desires, never the same.
Some people hope for riches
Of all life's earthly gain.

But when our hope is centered on God
He brings it all to pass.
The things that we do for Christ
Will satisfy and last.

Whatever your hopes and dreams may be,
Remember why Jesus came,
And give all the glory
And honor to His name.

It is so much more rewarding
When we set our hopes on high,
Knowing one day we'll see Jesus
And live after we die.

Written by
Lydia Carolyn Willoughby
© 1985

Psalms 31: 24
*"Be of good courage, and He shall strengthen
your heart, all ye that hope in the Lord."*

LIFE'S JOURNEY

I'd rather walk life's journey with Jesus
Knowing my path will always have light;
His radiance will scatter all darkness
Walking by faith and not by sight.

Some tasks when given may not be easy,
But if striving for heaven is an aim,
Then be willing to be a humble servant
Never to murmur or complain.

Sometimes it may hurt to do the right thing,
While trying, not always being the best,
But when we remain faithful
There is a reward when we pass the test.

So walk up the hills, through storms and low valleys
Winning souls, God's brilliant face to see,
And to wear that crown He has promised
A good and faithful servant at the end to be.

Written by
Lydia Carolyn Willoughby
© 8/23/12

2 Timothy 4:7
*"I have fought a good fight, I have finished
my course, I have kept the faith:"*

In Celebration of Ruth's Graduation on
Receiving her Ph.D. in Education

MY SISTER

Success is quite a journey,
A journey that never ends;
And those who travel with you
Are considered your true friends.
When you felt discouraged
And though your strength was gone,
God sent someone along your way
To give hope, to cheer you on.
Step by step, it's new you'll see.
New treasures will unfold,
And many good things will come to you
Because you have reached this goal.

Written by
Lydia Carolyn Willoughby
© 6/15/13

MY ANGEL

I was always with you.
I was present at your birth.
I was sent to you from heaven
To guide you everywhere on earth.

Do you remember your little dog, Lucky,
Who was your pet some years ago?
I sent him to be a companion.
He was that stray outside your door.

The days that I felt unhappy
Were those days others did you wrong;
I was with you when you felt lonely.
In the breeze I hummed a song.

When you were sick in the hospital
Every moment I was there.
I stood always by your bedside.
I supervised all your care.

The night I took you home to heaven
To family and friends, that was no fun,
But when Jesus called, you smiled and answered.
Now our work on earth is done.

Written by
Lydia Carolyn Willoughby
© 01/08/02

Psalms 34:7
"The angel of the Lord encampeth round about
them that fear Him and delivereth them."

WHEN I AWAKE

While not conscious as I sleep
With every breath and heartbeat,
It's not because of me I awake
But through God's grace and mercy's sake.
Places I go when in a dream
Though beautiful or scary they may seem,
I yet return to what is real
To thank the Lord for life that's frail,
For while I sleep, I could sleep on
Never to see another dawn.
But when I open my eyes to another day
It gives me another chance to pray.
I thank the Lord for life so sweet
On this earth each moment to greet

Every sunrise and sunset to adore
Each day I live to praise Him more.

Written by
Lydia Carolyn Willoughby
© 11/27/12

Psalms 71: 14
*"But I will hope continually, and will
yet praise Thee more and more."*

NO MORE TIME

I saw my casket on a grave
And oh, how sad,
Not because I died,
But because of all the time I had.

Time to do so many things
I had never done,
Taking for granted time with loved ones;
How I wish we had more fun.

My childhood hopes and dreams
When I was born,
My spirit wept out loud
Those opportunities now gone.

There were gifts I had to share
When I entered eternity's gate,
My whole life to review
It was too late.

They lower my body in the ground
And oh, that day my soul cried,
So many things I wanted to do
Before I died.

We pass this way but once.
Life is only just a glance.
Make the best of everyday;
Each moment could be a last chance.

Written by
Lydia Carolyn Willoughby
© 01/25/97

Psalm 90:12
"So teach us to number our days, that we
may apply our hearts unto wisdom."

REMEMBERING MOM'S SMILE

Mom, I'll miss your beautiful smile.
We walked together for your last mile.
My love for you will be the same.
Thank God you are no longer in pain.

Sometimes I feel so all alone,
Though I prayed for God to take you home,
Away from the suffering you've been through
To enter into a life that's new.

The clouds now in my life are gray.
I think of you, Mom, every day.
When I see the sunshine I'll remember your smile
And think of our parting as just for a little while.

Written by
Lydia Carolyn Willoughby
© 4/25/94

THE KEEPER OF THE LIGHTHOUSE

On a ship in the darkest night we sailed
As dark as it could be;
We drifted far away from shore
Not a single light to see.

Just then a storm arose
And tossed our ship from side to side.
By then we knew we wouldn't live;
We all would surely die.

But way out in the distance
I saw a speck of light;
We cried out loud to God
To safely bring us through the night.

I noticed as we prayed to God
The light drew very near
And suddenly we heard a voice
That spoke so soft and clear.

"Sin has caused this ship to drift
And you must sin no more,
But repent and follow me, the light,
And you'll safely reach the shore."

We obeyed and turned away from sin
And safely reached the land.
I noticed in the light house
Stood a tall and mighty man.

I walked up to the light house.
I could not behold his face.
The light was powerful as the sun,
Yet I felt such love and grace.

I said, "Dear Gentleman, it seems
You never get any rest."
He smiled and said, "No, my child,
Way north, south, east and west
Many ships will set out to sail
And some will lose their way,
So I cannot dare to rest, my child.
I work both night and day."

"Sir," I asked, "What is your name?"
He gently said to me,
"Jesus, the way, the truth, and the light:
The light for the world to see."

Written by
Lydia Carolyn Willoughby
© 1985

St. John 9: 5
*"As long as I am in the world, I
am the light of the world."*

FROM THIS DAY ON

I went to God in filthy rags
All torn and battered with sin.
I had no peace, no happiness
Nor any joy within.

Quietly I knelt praying;
My tears I could not hide.
He said, "What you need is Jesus
To love you and stand by your side."

I asked him, "Who is Jesus?"
He said, "Don't you know?
He is my precious holy son
Who died for you a long time ago."

He said I must confess my sins
And answer, "I do,"
To all of these questions
To live a life anew.

Would you accept Jesus in your heart?
To be Lord and Savior too?
To love honor and obey?
I answered, "Yes, I do."

In sickness or in health God said
He'll be with you all the way.
On life's hard road to travel
He'll hold your hand each day.

Do you promise to be faithful,
Earnest, and true?
With tears in my eyes and a humble heart
I answered, "Yes, I do."

I felt his love all around me.
My face was all aglow.
He renewed my mind and transformed my life
'til I was whiter than snow.
"I now pronounce you saved by grace."

Only heaven can understand.
I started down the aisles of life,
Jesus and I hand in hand.

Written by
Lydia Carolyn Willoughby
© 1983

John 3:16
*"For God so loved the world that He
gave His only begotten son,
That whosoever believeth in Him should not perish,
But have everlasting life."*

SATAN'S TRICK OR TREAT

Within the hand of Satan
Lies a bag with tricks or treats.
He'll come knocking at your door
To entice you to come and eat.

He always looks attractive
With that bag held in his hand;
He walks about the nations
Bringing death to every land.

One day I was spiritually hungry
And sat down to rest my feet.
Then came a knock outside my door
And a voice said, "Trick or treat."

But I heard another still soft voice
Saying, "You must study God's Holy Word."
But quickly I ran to the door
To that first voice I had heard.

There stood a man so handsome
He had that look in his eyes.
It was something strange about him
I should have known he was the father of lies.

Yet I opened my door to him
And welcomed him in.
Right then my spirit was broken
And my heart was full of sin.

He opened his bag of goodies
And out jumped the spirit of fear;
All the faith that God had given me
Was no longer there.

He then took out another package
And handed it to me.
In it said, "Now in bondage:
You are no longer set free."

There were many packages.
All were of defeat.
He took out a few little demons
Then left laughing, saying, "Trick or treat."

My life was in spiritual darkness.
I then had lost my way,
But I knew that Jesus loves me
And I remembered how to pray.

I got down on my knees that day
And asked Jesus to come in,
To wash me by his precious blood
From Satan's treats of sin.

The message in this poem
Is let God's word be your meat,
And you'll never be hungry
For the devil's trick or treat.

Written by
Lydia Carolyn Willoughby
© 11/10/88

Psalms 119:11
"Thy word have I hid in my heart that
I might not sin against Thee."

I wrote this poem especially for my
beloved mother's funeral.

CHERISH MEMORIES

Mummy earned a degree in MEEKNESS.
She earned a Master's degree in LOVE.
She earned another degree in KINDNESS
From her heavenly father above.

A special degree she held in PATIENCE;
To her Lord she lived true;
She earned a Ph.D. in FAITH
And one in LONG SUFFERING, too.

When we see the sun's bright light
We will see your smiling face.
You are our gem forever, a pearl
We will always embrace.

Along this journey of our lives
You've nourished us through the years.
You've been an example of God's love.
He will wipe away our tears.

When the gentle breezes blow
With songs from each little bird,
We'll think of the many songs you sang
And each kind spoken word.

When we see the pots and pans
Our hearts will take some time to heal,
When we remember all the times,
You prepared each delicious meal.

When we see the moon and stars
We will always think of you,
And know that you are with the Lord
Living a life that's new.

We'll always celebrate your life
In our hearts will ever be,
Bundles of treasured thoughts of you
As we cherish your memories.

Love you, Mummy.

Written by
Lydia Carolyn Willoughby
© 2004

Mrs. Millicent Willoughby
Went to be with the Lord September 19, 2004.
Rest in peace until we meet again.

GOD THE JUDGE

Before the jury reaches its verdict
In court, not another sound is heard
While everyone anxiously awaits
The judge's final word.

I watch the earthly lawyers
Pleading their client's case.
I see the expression at the moment
On a convicted person's face.

So will it be on the Judgment Day
Standing before God face to face,
To give an account of your earthly deeds
With no lawyer to plead your case.

If your life on earth wasn't pleasing to him
And your name not found in the book,
Any sinful act or idle word
He would not overlook.

Your sentence won't just be in prison
In some tiny cell,
But you'll be cast in the lake of fire
With the devil and his angels in hell.

But God's promise to His children
Is to walk on streets of gold,
With your names in the Lamb's Book of Life
Heaven's joy to unfold.

Now is your chance to accept the Lord Jesus
For tomorrow is no guarantee;
Now is the time to make the choice
Of where you'll spend eternity.

Written by
Lydia Carolyn Willoughby
© 1986

Romans 14:11, 12
*11. "For it is written, As I live, said the
Lord, every knee shall bow to me,
And every tongue shall confess to God.
12. So then every one of us shall give
account of himself to God."*

THE DAY JESUS KNOCKED
AT MY DOOR

I heard a gentle knock
One day outside my door.
I was so busy dusting;
Then I began to mop the floor.

Exhausted, I ran to open
As I whispered, "Who could this be?"
I didn't expect any company
For my place was a mess to see.

Though I slowly cleaned each corner
There was still dirt everywhere.
It was dark and filthy.
Then I began to pray.

I open the door. To my surprise
Stood a man radiant and bright.
I could never forget His precious smile
And I welcomed Him in that night.

He said, "I see you were trying
To clean this place alone;
You cannot do it by yourself
Only by my blood atone."

He said how much He loves me
I knew He spoke no lies,
Because the truth kept flowing.
I could see it in His eyes.

Without any hesitation,
All my sins to Him I confessed.
I never regret that moment
When to him I answered yes.

He said, "This place I'll keep spotless
And I promise I'll never part."
This place in which I welcomed him
Was deep within my heart.

Written by
Lydia Carolyn Willoughby
© 1986

Revelation 3:20
*"Behold I stand at the door and knock: if any man
hear my voice, and open the door, I will come in
to him, and will sup with him and he with me."*

MY ANGEL:
A SPIDER

I was called to fight in combat,
Across so many seas,
Where soldiers were killed or captured.
Fear drove me to my knees.

The fierceness of that battle
Left so many in despair,
Though I trusted in God's mercy
Yet I felt the presence of fear.

Some of my comrades were captured.
Somehow I managed to escape
Into a dark cave; I entered
Not knowing what could be my fate.

I heard the footsteps of my enemies
While I trembled in the cave.
I cried out to God to help me
So my life would be saved.

Just then I saw a spider.
I said, "God, how could this be
That you would send a spider
To come and rescue me?"

The spider quickly weaved a web
Across the cave's dark door,
As I crawled into a corner
On the hard and dusty floor.

I could hear my enemies talking
As they approached the cave that day.
A voice shouted, "No one can be inside.
There is a web across the entrance way!"

I heard them slowly leaving
As tears filled my eyes.
How a big God sent a little spider
Who was my angel in disguise.

With God, nothing is impossible.
Never despise whatever he brings.
He can help us move big mountains
With great or little things.

By God's grace and a spider's web,
In those moments how he cared!
By sending a little spider,
That's how my life was spared.

Written by
Lydia Carolyn Willoughby
© 12/03/08

Psalm 91: 5, 6, 7 & 11

5. *"Thou shalt not be afraid for the terror by night: nor for the arrow that flieth by day;* 6. *Nor for the pestilence that walketh in darkness; nor for the destruction that wasteth at noonday.* 7. *A thousand shall fall at thy side, and ten thousand at thy right hand; but it shall not come nigh thee. For He shall give his angel charge over thee to keep thee in all thy ways."*

MR. LONELINESS

Mr. Loneliness will pay a visit
And sometimes I just can't win;
When he comes knocking at my door
There are times I let him in.

He is ugly and ruthless
And really doesn't care.
He puts himself right on my walls;
That's when I begin to stare.

When he gets my full attention
He starts to tell me why,
The reason I feel all alone.
That's when he makes me cry.

I am single and familiar
With Mr. Loneliness.
He shows up where he is not welcomed
When I am not feeling my best.

When he comes to pay a visit
Everyone around can tell;
He also visits little children
And the elderly, as well.

I am learning how to cope with him
By occupying my time each day,
So I'll be always busy
When Mr. Loneliness comes my way.

Written by
Lydia Carolyn Willoughby
© 5/26/02

OVERCOMING THE FLESH

This flesh that I am close with
Is so weak and frail;
When my spirit wants to do what's right
I stumble and I fail.

I never put my trust in flesh,
Only God, for he is strong.
When I walk daily in His word
I am kept from doing wrong.

I cannot live for a moment
And never think I can
Live without God's guidance
And strength from His mighty hand.

I ask Him for forgiveness
When I think I've lost my way;
The flesh can be contrary
And can cause us to go astray.

But I thank God for His goodness
And mercies that bring me through;
Without Him when I have fallen.
I wouldn't know what to do.

Jesus knows all my weaknesses
Because He wore this flesh;
He knows it isn't easy
To stand up to the test.

He was often tried and tempted
With all life's physical needs,
Yet to God He remained faithful
And to sin He never yielded.

If only I could be like Him
Whose life on earth was pure,
Accepted and highly favored by God
Seated at His right hand for evermore.

Written by
Lydia Carolyn Willoughby
© 1984

Psalms 73:26
*"My flesh and my heart faileth: but God is the
strength of my heart, and my portion forever."*

Galatians 5:16 –
*"This I say then, walk in the spirit, and ye
shall not fulfil the lust of the flesh."*

JESUS, OUR PLACE OF REST

Way yonder on a hilltop
I gazed from a valley bleak;
There stood a little lowly house.
How I longed to rest my weary feet.

Through many thorns and thistles
In the dark I pressed on and on,
'til there was light before me;
It was a new day, a new dawn.

Many days I spent traveling.
Then up that hill I climbed,
Until I reached that little house.
I knocked; a voice spoke so kind.

"Come in, my weary traveler
Out of your toil and cares.
This house has been a refuge
For many, many years."

Inside stood a man clothed in white
With arms opened wide,
Such warmth of love, smiles and joy
That my tears I couldn't hide.

He led me to a table
And said, "My child, have a seat."
He asked God's blessings on the food;
Then we began to eat.

I knew that man was Jesus
For my soul was truly blessed;
When we get weary along life's way
In Jesus we can find REST.

Written by
Lydia Carolyn Willoughby
© 1986

Matthew 11:28
*"Come unto me, all ye that labour and are
heavy laden, and I will give you rest."*

THE SAVING BLOOD OF JESUS

I followed a crowd that was loud and angry;
We had no salvation and were doomed to loss.
We lived without hope; in tears I was frightened
While the crowd mocked three men on their cross.

But the cross that stood in the middle
Caught my attention right away.
Jesus so kind, so loving, and innocent
Was ready to be crucified that day.

The place called Golgotha was grim and dreary;
There were blood stains everywhere.
Unkind words were spoken to Jesus
As I watched in horror and trembled with fear.

I stood and watched those three men suffer;
Such cruelty I'll never understand.
Then they thrust a sword in the side of Jesus;
I heard them drive the nails in His hands.

He groaned in pain to His heavenly father.
To His heavenly father, only He cried,
"Father, please forgive them."
Then He gave up the ghost and died.

The earth stood still; His mockers ceased.
The sun refused to shine,
As we watched His final hour;
From heaven it was a sign.

At the cross there are priceless moments
Each drop of blood was shed for me,
And for the world salvation started
At Golgotha's blood-stained Calvary.

His death, was just the beginning
Of freedom from sin; I was a slave.
For by grace we can all be pardoned
Because He rose victorious from the grave.

Written by
Lydia Carolyn Willoughby
© 1985

Mark 14:24
"And He said unto them, this is my blood of the
New Testament which is shed for many".

THE TRUE CHURCH WITHOUT WALLS

I no longer look within a building
Of walls that we call the church;
For many years I've wondered
While my soul was in desperate search.

I clapped my hands and shouted
And worshipped God in praise;
I once sang in the choir
Yet I am still amazed.

To think that all along I thought
A church building was the only place,
That I could hear a word from God
Or kneel before His face.

With years of understanding
How to communicate with the Lord
Is to fellowship with him daily
With the spirit in one accord.

I learn about true worship
When I am feeling all alone
When family and friends are not around
God's presence is then made known.

When the doctor gave me a diagnosis
That I didn't want to hear,
I knew how to cry out to the Lord.
Thank God I knew how to pray.

The true church is the body of Christ
It may be far or near,
We are representatives of his kingdom
And we are everywhere.

Christ dwells within my temple;
I no longer have to search.
I take him with me everywhere
And when I go to church.

Written by
Lydia Carolyn Willoughby
Easter Sunday
© March 2, 2005

CHRISTIAN TRAFFIC LIGHTS AND SIGNS

On this narrow walk to heaven
Look for traffic lights and signs.
Always try to walk the straight way
Stay within the pure white lines.

At the amber light when approaching
Get ready to stop; stay always in prayer,
Because destruction may be before you
It's never the time to worry or fear.

Be patient when waiting at the red light;
Keep your feet within the lane.
Read God's word with faith and courage;
Green light signals go again.

When trying to cross a busy intersection
You may need to pray and fast,
For safety and God's divine direction
To stay always on the right path.

Though many will be going the broadways
And some from the Christian walk have left,
Only to see the sign, "Dead End"
That leads the way to sin and death.

Follow the "One Way" sign to Jesus.
Yield to him who is the Truth, Life and Way.
Beyond that sign points to heaven
Where we'll be caught up to meet
him one glorious day.

Written by
Lydia Carolyn Willoughby
© 1986

Proverbs 3:5, 6
5. *"Trust in the Lord with all thine heart; and*
lean not unto thine own understanding,
6. In all thy ways acknowledge Him
and He shall direct thy paths."

Matthew 7:14
"Because strait is the gate and narrow
is the way, which leadeth unto life,
and few there be that find it."

FOR OUR SENIORS

(1)   A life enriched with God's grace
And replenished with some tears
Is a Senior Citizen that's like an antique
With increased value over the years.

(2)   God has given you distinction.
Your hair that's now gray
Is a remarkable symbol of honor,
A silver crown to wear.

(3)   Life's learning comes with experience
And wisdom is the key
To God's knowledge and understanding
It's a blessing just to be –

(4)   An honorable senior citizen
With yet much work to do,
For there are teachers, leaders,
And counselors among you.

(5) The youth of today are searching,
And some are dying fast.
They need your help and encouragement
To help them along life's path.

(6) You may feel weak and tired
But don't sit only in a rocking chair.
That life to you God has given
Has something for you to share.

(7) You are our prized possessions,
Remember, crowned with honor and grace,
So work until Jesus calls you.
Help others run this race.

Written by
Lydia Carolyn Willoughby
© 09/20/96

A NEW BABE IN CHRIST

I am a newborn babe in Christ
In the precious sight of God,
Accepted in His blessed fold
Protected by His staff and rod.

As a lamb I am frail and tender,
But for redemption to the cross I came.
I heard the voice of my loving shepherd
When He gently called my name.

This spiritual walk I am now beginning,
God's Word is what I need
To help me live the Christian life
When on His word I feed.

Each day I am growing stronger
From a healthy life of prayer.
One day I'll be a mature Christian
With my heavenly father's care.

Written by
Lydia Carolyn Willoughby
© 1985

1 Peter 2:1, 2
*"Wherefore laying aside all malice, and all
guile, and hypocrisies, and envies and all evil
speakings, as newborn babes, desire the sincere
milk of the word, that ye may grow thereby."*

A DIRECT DIAL TO JESUS

You need to give Jesus a call
And talk with Him every day
Whether the sun is shining
Or your blue skies turn to gray.

You will never hear a recording
Saying, "Press 1, 2, or 3,"
If you want to talk to Jesus,
And, by the way, all calls are free.

There is never a busy signal.
The lines are always clear.
No charge for extra minutes
And you can call from anywhere.

Jesus is always listening
For phone calls every day.
Miraculous things can happen
When we go to God in prayer.

No cables needed for communication
Only to be humble and sincere
A direct dial to Jesus
Is just a matter of words in prayer.

Written By
Lydia Carolyn Willoughby
© 1985

BEWARE OF SATAN'S LOOK-ALIKES

There are so many look-alikes
In our world today;
We must use wisdom
And always watch and pray.

The devil is tricky.
He makes things seem so right.
He is the angel of darkness,
But appears as one of light.

Be not anxious in anything.
Seek God diligently.
Let him direct you;
Try the spirit and see.

Now Satan isn't very smart,
And if you have spiritual sight,
You'll know if something is from God
Or one of his look-alikes.

Written by
Lydia Carolyn Willoughby

© 1985

1 John 4:1
"Beloved, believe not every spirit, but try the
spirits whether they are of God: because many
false prophets are gone out into the world."

GOD CAN TURN IT AROUND

When you are in a struggle
With your back against a wall
And darkness all around
Like you are going to fall,

You'll never go under to cross over
As long as in Jesus you abide.
Trusting in him always,
You'll safely reach the other side.

The joy that awaits you
After all the clouds and rain!
Keep believing in God's promise
That the sun will shine again.

It doesn't matter the situation
That keeps your spirit bound.
Let go and let God have His way;
He can surely turn it around.

Written by
Lydia Carolyn Willoughby
© 1985

Psalms: 46:1
*"God is our refuge and strength, a
very present help in trouble."*

I'LL FLY

The caterpillar with nowhere else to go
Its world and time move very slow
Upon a leaf or a tree limb;
The bright sunshine seems very dim.

Motionless lies its pupal case
An example of God's love and grace.
With hope ahead through the dark gloom
Is a life of change in one cocoon.

Each passing moment when to find
It's only for a season and a matter of time
That change will take place and hope will be
A beautiful butterfly for the world to see.

The caterpillar sees its end on earth
As just the beginning to a new birth.
The welcomed change, what joy it brings
When a butterfly is given its colorful wings!

This miracle of change does have some pain
Never wanting to be a caterpillar again,
Bidding the cocoon's world goodbye.
Now to have the courage to believe, to fly.

Dear God, you made the caterpillar
With the change that it goes through.
Whenever I see a butterfly
I see the beauty in you.

Written by
Lydia Carolyn Willoughby
© 08/24/1999

*"What the caterpillar calls the end of the
world, the master calls a butterfly."*
quote by Richard Bach

Job 14:14
*"If a man dies, shall he live again? All the days of
my appointed time will I wait till my change come."*

HEARTBREAK CITY

I went to a place called "Heartbreak City"
Where the streets are watered every day with tears.
I walked down a street called
"Disappointment and Rejection."
All the streets were named after burdens and cares.

I saw a place where men and women were separated;
Their children were tormented by an evil force.
I felt so sad to see so many people hurting.
I looked at the street sign; it read, "Divorce."

I walked a little further to a gloomy pathway,
To a little street that caught my eyes.
The sign read, "Molestation and Depression."
That was when I began to cry.

When I saw all the little children,
Men, women and babies, too,
That were abused by their loved ones and others
I prayed to God to see us through.

I was surprised while in "Heartbreak City"
To see many rich folks from the hall of fame,
Though they lived on a street just for the elite,
Their hearts were filled with pain.

So many had put their trust in people
And had no trust in God above.
There were so many single people
Hurt deeply by the ones they loved.

The reason I was in "Heartbreak City"
Was, to myself I must be true,
I felt alone; I was rejected.
You see, my heart was broken, too.

But in God's Word I found hope and comfort.
The Holy Spirit helped me to realize
That a broken and a contrite heart
God said He will not despise.

I prayed as I kept on walking
Though my flesh was feeling weak.
I saw a sign that read, "Deliverance,"
So I started down that street.
Faith kept me every day believing
'til Jesus took me by the hand
And led me out of "Heartbreak City"
Into a place called "Victory Land."

No matter how much your heart's been broken
Trust in the Lord; He'll make a way.
Look for the sign that reads, "Deliverance,"
And move out of "Heartbreak City" today.

Written by
Lydia Carolyn Willoughby
© 08/24/2012

Psalm 51:17
*"The sacrifices of God are a broken spirit: a broken
and a contrite heart, O God, thou will not despise."*

Psalms 147:3
*"He healeth the broken in heart and
bindeth up their wounds."*

Psalms: 34:18
*"The Lord is nigh unto then that are of a broken
heart; and saveth such as be of a contrite spirit."*

DON'T WAIT TO SAY, "I'M SORRY."

Life is like a vapor
As fragile as can be.
Every moment passing
Is just a memory.

Its ups and downs and trials
Are a part of life along the way.
We sometimes have misunderstandings
From things we do or say.

But forgiveness is a valuable key
That unlocks the door to peace.
When there is an opportunity
Don't let that moment cease.

To say the words, "I am sorry,"
And mean it from the heart,
As the dawning of each day
Can be a fresh new start.

We pass this way so quickly.
To live in peace is less worry.
Let's not wait until it's too late
To want to say, "I am sorry."

Written by
Lydia Carolyn Willoughby
© 07/14/2011

Ephesians 4:32
"And be kind one to another tenderhearted,
Forgiving one another even as God for
Christ's sake hath forgiven you."

James 4:14
"Whereas ye know not what shall be on the morrow,
For what is your life? It is even a vapor,
that appeareth for a little time,
And then vanisheth away."

IF THE TRAIN WERE THE RAPTURE

One morning I was running late.
All that was my aim,
While walking to the station
Was to catch that eight o'clock train.

I hastened up the stairs and whispered,
"Lord, please give me a chance,
Though I am late to catch this train,"
Then I took a glance.

It was already at the station.
I was exhausted from running up the stairs,
But what a joy, just to know
That in everything, God cares.

The conductor saw me coming;
At the opened door he stood.
I entered the train saying a prayer,
"Thank you, Lord, you are so good."

If this were the rapture
I couldn't for a moment wait.
There I would stand with the door closed
Because of one moment too late.

Written by
Lydia Carolyn Willoughby
© 1984

Matthew 25:10
"And while they went to buy,
The bridegroom came; and they that were ready
Went in with him to the marriage
and the door was shut."

LITTLE IS MUCH

Little is much when God is in it.
It doesn't matter what it is,
It's a joy just to be in his favor
To know always that we are his.

Some doors he opens may seem little
And some not like our comfort zone,
But by faith and trust in his great wisdom
Those doors will just be a stepping stone.

Give thanks always for humble beginnings.
Everything God gives is blessed.
He watches how we take care of little things;
Sometimes it's only a test.

It's never easy in any struggle
But remember to give thanks every day.
Little is much when God is in it
Out of little things he can make a big way.

Written by
Lydia Carolyn Willoughby
© 07/12/2006

Psalm 37:16; Luke 19:17

GOD SEES

God sees those who are hungry,
And he loves the poor.
He daily sees the homeless
Looking for an open door.

He loves people of all races,
If considered of high or low degree.
Whoever is in bondage,
He wants to set them free.

God sees dying souls
Everywhere in each land.
He wants so much to work through us
To lend a helping hand.

He sees the single parent
Who has no help at home.
He sees hearts that are broken;
He sees those who eat alone.

God sees weary prisoners
And time after time,
He visits behind those bars
To forgive every crime.

He sees and knows everything
And understands every situation.
That's why He sent His son to die
To give us full salvation.

He sees those labeled as outcasts
From society,
He wants to help because he cares
For all humanity.

Written by
Lydia Carolyn Willoughby
© 1986

Psalm 66:7
*"He ruleth by His power forever; His
eyes behold the nations: let not the
rebellious exalt themselves."* Selah.

HAVE YOU INVITED JESUS TODAY?

I was invited to a special service
On a friends and family day.
My family members weren't around
But I attended anyway.

There were lots of smiling faces
Of members, old and new.
I thought everyone invited Jesus
But those who did were few

I had prayed that morning early.
This was my prayer request:
I asked Jesus to go with me
To be my friend and family guest.

He sat with me through the service.
He watched all the formality.
He listened to every spoken word,
And then he looked at me.

I noticed there were tears in his eyes.
I asked him what was wrong.
He said, "My servant preached my word,
And I enjoyed each song.

But my heart is still so heavy
For these souls that are gathered here,
Just a few remembered to
Invite me in a prayer.

It's not that they didn't invite me
That concerns me the most
It's that so few have accepted me,
My father, and the Holy Ghost.

You see I paid so great a price
For everyone's free salvation,
My blood left stains on Calvary
To secure their home in heaven."

Don't forget to invite Jesus
In your hearts to stay
And make Him your special guest
On this friends and family day.

Written by
Lydia Carolyn Willoughby © 08/08/93

This poem was written for a Friends
and Family service in New Jersey.

GOD'S DIVINE POWER

It took God's divine power
To part the great Red Sea,
And deliver the Israelites out of bondage
From Egypt to set them free.

It is His divine power
That allows the sun to shine,
The moon and the stars at night,
And water made into wine.

Again it was God's divine power
When five thousand people were fed,
With just five loaves and two fishes
And Lazarus risen from the dead.

His might and divine power
Made whole again Jarius's daughter.
Jesus too was risen from the grave
And he also walked on water.

In God is our hope and strength
A strong and mighty tower
Let us with his praises sing
For His divine wisdom and power.

Written by
Lydia Carolyn Willoughby
© 2007

Romans 13:1
"Let every soul be subject unto the higher powers.
For there is no power but of God.
The powers that be are ordained of God."

OUR WISE GOD

God is too wise
To make a mistake.
His diligence and power
And knowledge are great.

Our lack of understanding
And thoughts are too small;
We cannot compare,
For He ruleth over all.

He knows the future;
He can hinder or allow.
His sight goes beyond
The present our now.

His will towards us
Is for always the best.
There is a profound reason
For His "No," "Wait," or "Yes."

He cares with compassion
Like a loving father should
And finds pleasure in blessing
Us only with good.

When Satan, a roaring lion,
Comes around in disguise
He guards and protects us
With His divine eyes.

So always remember
Our heavenly father, so Great,
Is too wise in His knowledge
To make a mistake.

Written by
Lydia Carolyn Willoughby
© 09/24/2003

Romans 16:27
"To God only wise, be glory
Through Jesus Christ forever. Amen."

TRUE LOVE

Unconditional love has no price tag;
It's not known as rich or poor.
Its element attracts the soul and spirit
Leading to an open door.

True love is not fake
And requires no perfection.
Its worth and value stays the same.
It never grows weary or tired of sharing.

It doesn't seek beauty;
It doesn't seek fame.
It's selfless and caring and always transparent,
Feeling one's joy and also one's pain.

Never swift to highlight faults of others,
And will find it hard to expose their shame.
But rather uplift for it cherishes the soul.
True love is more precious than silver or gold.

So if you are blessed to meet one with such love
Always remember that's a gift from above.

Written by
Lydia Carolyn Willoughby
© 02/14/2009
On Valentine's Day

SOME ORDINARY PEOPLE ON GOD'S WALL OF FAME

There was a poor humble girl;
Mary was her name.
She was simple in every way,
But she reached God's wall of fame.

Above all women you may think
It to be an impossible thing,
That this insignificant, quiet girl
Was the mother of the greatest king.

Moses was on the backside of a mountain
Never knowing his life would be
A great leader that God had chosen
To lead his people out of captivity.

Esther raised up in an orphanage
Was a poor, lonely girl.
Became a queen highly favored,
Her story known all over the world.

Joseph was thrown in a well by his brothers,
Was sold as a slave but in due time
Became one of the greatest rulers in Egypt
And to his brothers was loving and kind.

While in the field David praised God in worship.
He played his harp, he loved to sing.
He was just a shepherd boy in the eyes of people,
But in God's eyes, he was always a king.

On God's wall of fame are ordinary people
With an earthly mission, God's work to fulfill.
He can choose the quiet, unnoticed, and humble
To show His glory, to implement His will.

Written by
Lydia Carolyn Willoughby
© 08/29/2000

Matthew 20:16
"So the last shall be first and the first last;
for many be called but few chosen."

SORRY, WORRY, AND FAITH

I met three outstanding people
While walking along life's way.
I met a man called, "Sorrow."
He kept looking back that day.

While walking a very busy street
And as I looked around
I met a man named, "Worry."
On his face there was a frown.

Down the road a little further
I met Mr. Faith and I could see
He was looking up towards heaven
For his hope and victory.

Sorrow looks back in the past,
Worry looks around,
But Faith looks towards heaven
For his hope, stars, and crown.

Written by
Lydia Carolyn Willoughby
© 10/06/97

Hebrews 11: 1
*"Now faith is the substance of things hoped
for, the evidence of things not seen."*

THE DIVINE MATCHMAKER

There are many Christian singles
Who are looking everywhere
For that someone very special
To love and their lives to share.

"It seems almost impossible
To find the right one," they say,
But God gives us the desires of our hearts
When we walk in His way.

You may think you are not beautiful,
Handsome, or even smart.
But God doesn't see these things;
He looks only at the heart.

He is the divine matchmaker;
On Him you can rely.
He knows just who is right for you.
You'll be beautiful in that someone's eye.

You may have prayed and are still waiting
Not seeing an answer yet;
He is preparing you for that special one.
Be patient; you'll never regret.

He always hears and answers
When on His name we call.
If you are waiting for your husband or wife,
He is the best matchmaker of them all.

Written by
Lydia Carolyn Willoughby
© 1986

Matthew 21:22
*"And all things, whatsoever ye shall
Ask in prayer believing ye shall receive."*

SERVING THE LORD

I always wanted to serve the Lord
So I prayed earnestly;
I said, "Dear Lord, show me the way
To best worship and serve thee."

One day as I was walking,
Along came a poor, old man.
He asked me if I had some extra change,
But instead I held back my hand.

That day along came a little girl
Who seemed to have lost her way,
But I was very busy
And that little girl went astray.

Then along came a lady crying.
She seemed frightened and alone.
Some belongings she was carrying
Like she was evicted from her home.

I thought serving the Lord was going to church
And that night when I knelt to pray,
God said, "My heart is very sad.
You turned me three times away."

He said, "I didn't come in the way
That you expected to see."
Then I realized He can come
In people like you and me.

I asked Him to forgive me
And to help me serve as best I can.
In serving others we serve the Lord.
We are his mouth, ears, eyes, feet and hands.

Written by
Lydia Carolyn Willoughby
© 1985

Romans 12:10, 11
*"10. Be kindly affectioned one to another
with brotherly love; in honour preferring
one another; 11. Not slothful in business;
fervent in spirit; serving the Lord."*

THE KEY TO YOUR HEART

When you give first place to God above
He will teach you all the secrets of love.
The heart is a very sacred place
And can only be kept by His love and grace.

He has given to us desires to fulfill,
If we want His best we, must be in His will.
Let God direct and choose the day
When you can give that key away.

So many of us are broken and alone.
When Satan gets the key, many hearts are torn,
Give your key to Jesus and let it remain.
It will save a lot of heartache and pain.

He alone knows all that we need;
Trust Him always and let Him lead.
If your heart's been broken, he can give a fresh start.
Don't give to anyone the key to your heart.

Written by
Lydia Carolyn Willoughby
© 2001

VALUED TIME

Every second the clock is ticking
And we are getting older still.
Put time and effort into things of value
Each moment to maximize and fulfill.

Say things to enchant a smile or laughter;
Reminisce on the things that make the heart glad.
Focus on the positive not the negative;
Talk about the good and not the bad.

There is nothing we can do about the aging process
When our hair in exchange for black grows gray.
And things we could once do become difficult
With aches and pains from life's wear and tear.

On youth we simply cannot bargain,
And on beauty we can never rely.
I view our lives as a field of flowers,
We flourish, bloom, and then we die.

When we are gone it doesn't have to be final.
Now is important what we do with our time.
It can be spent creating a legacy
For those that we will leave behind.

Psalms 90:12
*"So teach us to number our days, that
we may apply our hearts unto wisdom."*

Written by
Lydia Carolyn Willoughby
© 05/03/08

THE CAGED EAGLE

It was an unfortunate circumstance
That a poor eagle could not fly.
He stayed in a cage with other birds
And some days they watched him cry.

You see he lost his Mother
When he was just a baby bird.
He wasn't taught how to use his wings
And every day this is what he heard.

"You'll never be able to use those wings,
So get used to walking in the dust.
Forget those beautiful mountain tops,
For you are now one of us."

But deep inside that eagle's heart
He knew, that was not true;
He believed there was something greater
That he was created to do.

So one day he tried to show them
When he was let out of the cage.
He flew not high and fell to the ground;
He realized it was because of his age.

He wings were never developed
But he was determined to try.
They laughed each time he fell to the ground,
Yet he still believed he could fly.

That eagle never quit trying.
His vision always a mountain top.
Over and over he failed and tried;
His determination was never to stop.

His instinct led him to a place
Where in his heart he knew
That he had to ignore the mocking,
The laughing, and criticism, too.

He used his wings to comfort others;
That eagle knew how to pray.
While waiting for his change to come
He helped others along the way.

One day he looked up in the sky
And thought it seemed so odd,
He saw a hand that beckoned to him,
It was the hand of God.

His attention on it was focused
Forgetting the negative things.
His eyes were fastened on that hand.
Faith helped him spread his wings.

He noticed that he did not fall
Nor his wings did not flop.
God took him right to his dream:
A beautiful mountain top.

With tears he then looked down to see
How he had flown so high.
In his heart he always believed
It's never too late to fly.

Written by
Lydia Carolyn Willoughby
© 08/25/2014

Mark 9:23
*"Jesus said unto him, if thou canst believe all
things are possible to him that believeth."*

"Through it all, I learned to trust in
Jesus I learned to trust in God,
Through it all I learned to depend upon his word."
Quote by Andre Crouch

LABORING FOR THE MASTER

When I enter a room
Do I expel the gloom?
Or do I think about myself
Instead of putting me on a shelf?

Am I an excellent host
Used by God with the Holy Ghost?
Do I loosen my face
With a beautiful smile of grace?

This work doesn't seek fame
And isn't all about financial gain,
Sometimes sweaty and stressed
Yet striving to do my best.

It may not be pretty at all
When we answer to God's call.
Do you really want to serve the Lord
And receive your special reward?

Then learn to serve others
In a way that is right.
Light that special candle
That will burn in this dark night.

So if you are willing,
God's got a place reserve,
For you to help others
In his kingdom to serve.

Written By
Lydia Carolyn Willoughby
© 08/12/2014

MY LIFE PREACHES

I preach a sermon by the way I live.
I preach a sermon by how I give.
I preach a sermon by sharing a word or song.
I preach a sermon even when things go wrong.

I preach a sermon by the way I walk.
I preach a sermon by the way I talk.
I preach a sermon when I believe God through a test.
I preach a sermon even by the way I dress.

I preach a sermon so others, Jesus will know.
I preach a sermon everywhere I go.
I preach a sermon so people can see
The greatest sermon preached at Calvary.

At that place wasn't the spoken word
But the nails driven in his hands are what they heard.
Our Christian walk is what we do
That lets the world know we are faithful and true.

Every day of our lives we must take heed
Because we are the only Bible that some people read.

Written by
Lydia Carolyn Willoughby
© 09/28/2014

DEATH'S VISIT

Death is unfriendly and very cold.
His visit hurts young and old.
It doesn't matter who we are;
Death causes a wound that leaves a scar.

He comes any hour, day or night,
With his sting and with his bite,
He causes us to be apart
Leaving behind a bleeding heart.

For his visit we can never be prepared,
A visit that we all have feared,
Short life or long life will always be
Death at our doorstep we will see.

But Jesus who is always near
Gives comfort through our friends who care,
To know after this life is a reward,
Just to fall asleep in the arms of the Lord.

So that void we feel when all alone
Still to rejoice a loved one has gone home,
Through the heartache and through the pain
Lies hope that we will meet again.

Written by
Lydia Carolyn Willoughby
© 09/18/2014

MEASURING SUCCESS

If I have everything to my heart's content,
All in life I can possess.
I ask the question, "Will it all measure up
To what we call success?"

To be highly favored by those we know
Away from worries and stress,
Or to have many degrees that cover the wall,
Is that living life at its best?

When we meet the needs of others
A purpose for all to live,
A consciousness of love and caring
When we find in our hearts to give,

Finding the hidden key to success
Is to be centered in God's will,
And with his unmerited favor
Our life's purpose to fulfill.

If there be any lives we have touched
Along this life's pathway,
Then success is measured in thoughtful things
We do for others every day.

Written by
Lydia Carolyn Willoughby
© 09/01/2014

I LOST MY LOVE TO ALZHEIMER'S

It seems like only yesterday
Our lives were such a different way.
We talked, we laughed, we hugged and cuddled.
This terrible disease began so subtle.

I shed some tears almost every day
Where I find a secret place to pray.
I bleed inside; my weary soul melts
It feels to me you are someone else.

Present times you quickly forget;
It's like you are not the same person I met.
I still always believe your thoughts are with me now,
But you take me back in the past somehow.

Asking the same questions over and over again,
It's not your fault, Honey, Alzheimer's is to blame.
That's when I take you by the hand
To let you know I understand.

You seldom ever remember my name,
But the love I have for you will always be the same.
Each moment in this storm with life's rough tide
As long as I live, I'll be always by your side.

Written by
Lydia Carolyn Willoughby
© 09/23/2014

ENJOY LIFE

Life is so short,
Spend some time to laugh.
Forget the worries;
Leave off some tasks.

Kick off your shoes.
Enjoy an ocean breeze.
Although life can be tough,
In it, find some ease.

When it is raining,
Don't say it's a nasty day.
Just find a tune to dance in it;
Find some time to play.

Time is swiftly passing.
Look for things that bring joy to do.
Take pictures of a sunset
Or from a mountain view.

Spend time with friends and family,
And this list could go on and on.
Regard your time as quality
Before it is all gone.

Written by
Lydia Carolyn Willoughby
© 06/24/2014

DIAL 1-800-FORGIVE

When someone has hurt you
It's often hard to forgive.
You can hold on to grudges
For as long as you live.

Un-forgiveness only creates
Bitterness in the heart,
Un-happiness and anger
That keep family and friends apart.

But forgiveness brings freedom
That always releases the soul.
Such freedom is worth
More than money, silver, or gold.

Being forgiving is not easy.
Start by going to God in prayer.
It will lift that heavy burden
And relationship repair.

In your heart, dial the number of Jesus.
He will teach you how to live.
It is toll free: just believe
1-800 FORGIVE.

Written by
Lydia Carolyn Willoughby
© 06/23/2014

NO! TOO BUSY, GOD

God handed me a package of gifts
a long time ago.
I placed them on a shelf;
their value I didn't know.

I was a Straight "A" student
and in college I gained a degree,
But there was something missing,
an emptiness in me.

I went to church to worship God
and as I bowed to pray,
I asked the Lord to help me find
the joy that wasn't there.

One Sunday after church
the pastor asked if I would teach
the children in Sunday school
or help with the youth outreach.

I said, "Dear Pastor, as you know
my schedule is so tight."
Then he asked, "What about the midweek service?"
I replied, "No time at night."

Again the pastor came to me
and asked if I would lead
in prayer some Sunday mornings
or the Scripture lesson read.

The years rolled on; my husband passed;
my children all left home.
The emptiness I feel inside
now that I am all alone.

I made so many excuses;
all these years I made God wait.
I wish I had answered to His call;
now I realize it's way too late.

I turned to Him for inner peace.
He said, "Look on the shelf."
My sight is now failing
and I am in poor physical health.

I opened the package of gifts
for the first time in many years.
One gift was the gift of singing;
I broke down that night in tears.

Another was the gift of teaching
to bless and encourage lost souls.
But I was just too busy
reaching my selfish goals.

That night I asked the Lord to forgive me
though I didn't do His will.
He put His loving arms around me
I know He loves me still.

The message in this poem
is your purpose brings reward.
You live a life filled with blessings
when you use your gifts for the Lord.

Written by
Lydia Carolyn Willoughby
© 1996

MY PURPOSE AS A WEED

Upon the river bank I cleave
Where pretty flowers bloom.
I am another weed unknown
To find my purpose soon.

I watch each flower as it goes
To the filing of someone's eye,
With attracted beauty of color and flare
And often wonder why.

I suffer so much rejection
While their fragrance fills the air
And cry the tears of loneliness
As I watch them disappear.

I am a weed but still a plant
In a world of my own.
God fashioned me; he has a plan.
To me, it's not yet known.

Will capture into someone's eyes
My value and my worth.
I know there is a purpose
For everything on earth.

Written by
Lydia Carolyn Willoughby
© 2000

JESUS THE LIGHT

Words sometimes are just not enough,
When hearts are broken, when times are tough.
When tears fall from our eyes like rain,
And nothing seems to soothe the pain.
But when Jesus shows up on the darkest day,
He comes with light to lead the way.
And every storm at His command,
Will cease to roar as He holds our hand.
And shelters with His love and grace,
That comforts with His warm embrace.

Written by
Lydia Carolyn Willoughby
© 3/26/15

THIS POEM WAS WRITTEN FOR MY PARENTS 50TH WEDDING ANNIVERSARY

Whoso findeth a wife findeth a good thing, and obtaineth favour of the Lord. Proverbs 18:22

While walking through this path called life,
A man named Clyde found a beautiful wife.
"He who finds a wife finds a good thing;"
She is the pride of her home, and
makes her husband a king.

He searched before and did not find
a woman so gracious, so precious, and kind.
A jewel found among diamonds and pearls,
an excellent mother of three boys and four girls.

Her voice in his ears is what embraced his heart.
Their love for each other is a master piece of art.
They've journeyed together for fifty long years;
Through happiness, through heartache,
with laughter and tears.

He stood by her side when sickness came.
Though she became disabled; he loved her the same.
From a Godly foundation this marriage was formed.
They walked hand in hand and
weathered each storm.

For God's love and faithfulness
we owe him the praise;
For blessing this marriage for fifty long years.
A covenant, a commitment, from
two hearts that are true.
From Esther, Eunice, Ruth, Clyde Jr.,
Lydia, and John, and Andrew,
We all love you!

Written by
Lydia Carolyn Willoughby
© June 2000

A PRAYER

Lord, give me a short term memory
Only when people do me wrong.
That I can go on loving
With praises and a song.
Not nurturing painful memories
That stir up confusion and strife.
That would cause me to forfeit
Living a victorious Christian life.
One exemplified of Christ
For without Him I cannot live.
Until I learn the secret to joy
When I learn to forgive.

Written by
Lydia Carolyn Willoughby
© 6/23/15

A PRAYER

Great God of this universe,
To you is this prayer without rehearse.
I praise you now as God alone
For creating this world and many yet unknown.
I thank you for Jesus, whose blood flows free
For every sinner in this world and me.
I thank you, gracious Father, for all that you do,
And for the Holy Spirit, whose friendship is true.
Thank you for mercy and grace every day,
That I can live by faith, come what may.
Knowing I am safe walking in your divine will
At last to the end, my purpose to be fulfilled
Then to behold the beauty of your face
After I have finished life's toil, my earthly race.
I long to be in your presence, I long to be with you
And all of heaven's family to live life anew.

Written by
Lydia Carolyn Willoughby
© 5/23/15

A PRAYER

Lord, as long as you are my guiding light,
I'll trust when in darkness, though
it may seem not right.
The road may be bumpy walking a narrow lane,
But I'll stretch my faith with uncertainty or pain.
Hoping for joy in the morning while
my night has been long,
By faith walking with you, I can never go wrong.
Knowing your timing is right and
always worth the wait,
You are an on-time God; that
means you are never late.

Written by
Lydia Carolyn Willoughby
© 6/29/15

POSITIVE PERFORMANCE

Positive performance is to be at work on time,
To be always devoted, trustworthy, and kind.

Never to be tardy but hard-working and true,
Committed and consistent in all that you do.

Excellent in job performance,
and always willing to be,
A part of progressing to your best ability.

Your outward appearance plays a very big part, too,
To be well-groomed and ready, your duties to do.

Positive performance must achieve nothing less
Than your reaching that goal
always to be your very best.

Written by
Lydia Carolyn Willoughby
© 1990

A WOMAN WITH ISSUE OF BLOOD

Her name was never mentioned.
Her story, a legacy,
One of fathomless faith
Told in biblical history.

She knew what scorn was all about
As she suffered twelve long years.
I believe she bore a lot of shame and
Rejection while crying many tears.

Seeking help from many physicians
With no hope, how sad
While all promised her healing
Taking all the funds she had.

Being unclean no man could take her
To be a lawful wife
This was a part of her rejection
She suffered twelve years of her life.

But one day she heard about Jesus
And the power of His name.
She believed that if she pressed her way
She would be whole again.

Though the crowd would not allow her,
She pressed as she kneeled
Just to touch the hem of Jesus' garment.
That's how the woman was healed.

Virtue immediately left Jesus
For her faith had made her bold.
Jesus cured her of her plague;
From that hour she was made whole.

Whatever issue in life you have,
With faith to Jesus give
Every burden of your heart.
Look now to Him and live.

Written by
Lydia Carolyn Willoughby
© 6/16/15

Matthew 9:20, 21; Mark 5: 25-34; Luke 8: 43-48

*"And, behold, a woman, which was diseased
with an issue of blood twelve years, came behind
him, and touched the helm of his garment:
For she said within herself, if I may but
touched his garment, I shall be whole."*

A LITTLE MUSCULAR ORGAN

There is a little organ;
Between the teeth is its house.
It can be loud and dangerous
Or quiet as a mouse.

It can transmit love and kindness.
It can be a deadly weapon, too.
It can cause war or peace;
So much that little organ can do.

Its power generates from the heart.
It can bring forth death or life.
It can be like a healing balm
Or can cut just like a knife.

We must always be mindful
Of every word we say,
For we all must give an account
To God on the Judgment Day.

This little muscular organ
In every mouth is found
With pink tissue and thousands of taste buds,
None other than the tongue.

Written by
Lydia Carolyn Willoughby
© 6/16/15

Matthew 12:36
*"But I say unto you, that every idle word
that men shall speak they shall give account
thereof in the day of Judgment."*

ACKNOWLEDGEMENTS
AND DEDICATIONS

I thank God first and foremost for graciously guiding me along this path, for picking me up each time I fall, and for blessing me with the assurance of His love.

This book is a dedicated to the sacred memory of my precious parents, the late Rev. and Mrs. Clyde Willoughby, who taught my siblings and me to fear the Lord.

This extends to my siblings: Rev. Esther Willoughby; Eunice Willoughby-Forde; Dr. Ruth Hinkson; Clyde Willoughby, Jr.; John Willoughby; and Andrew Willoughby, Attorney-at-Law, and my nieces, nephews, and in-laws.

It is with grateful appreciation that I acknowledge the contributions of my sister, Rev. Esther Willoughby, who gave me strong support by planting seeds towards this book by having Ms. Lydia Carter who typed the poems. Thank you, Lydia. You did an excellent job and

Mrs. Sandra Cadogan, who is a friend of Esther, who did some editing.

My sister, Dr. Ruth Hinkson, has been a great inspiration and encouragement; she also helped in the layout of this book. To my sister, Mrs. Eunice Willoughby-Forde, who did some preliminary editing, along with my nephew, Jamal Hinkson, Attorney-at-Law, whose technical skills were of great assistance and Dr. Lesley Scharf who did the final editing; Thank you Dr. Scharf, you did a terrific job.

My appreciation is extended to Reverend Dr. Joel Cumberbatch, who was pastor of the Whitepark Wesley Holiness Church, for always giving me an opportunity to share some of my poems with his congregation whenever I visited Barbados. He is now superintendent of the Wesleyan Holiness Church in the Caribbean.

In loving memory of the late Rev. Beatrice Phillips, who for many years was a friend and mentor. May she rest peacefully from all her life's labors.

To some very special friends of mine: Mrs. Marlene Skinner of New York; Ms. Louise Waker of New Jersey; Ms. Daphne Martin of New Jersey; Mrs. Muriel Worrell of Barbados; Mrs. Tricia Mitchell of Florida, whose prophetic word propelled me to the finishing line, and Mrs. Ernesta Mcpherson of Barbados, for planting a seed that will not be forgotten. Thank you all for your love and prayers.

I also wish to remember my pet cat Sweetie who loved me through my pain and joy, and to my beautiful pet cat Snow White who likes to sit with me when I write. Love you all!

ABOUT THE AUTHOR

I do believe that God gives us gifts and talents. It is always a blessing when we can use them for the building of His Kingdom. I have the innate ability to communicate effectively when I put my deepest thoughts and feelings into words. My passion is writing poetry. My personal experience came about in inspiring others when I received raving reviews from listeners after I read three of my poems as a guest on the New Life radio program, Voice of Barbados while visiting with family. The host of that program is Rev. Esther Willoughby, my sister. I had two of my poems published in magazines and one on the CEO's blog at my job. I was also given the honor to read some of them at various functions. Along my life's journey and walk of faith, I've experienced the mighty hand of God which inspired me to write. My love for Him is an expression in poetry. I am a native of Bridgetown, Barbados, and after living in New York and New Jersey for some years, I currently reside in Florida. I am a care giver for many years. My love for the Lord is also serving others. My hobbies are singing, playing the piano and guitar, and writing.

Printed in the United States
By Bookmasters